The Great Littl
of
Revision & Showing You Know

Essential, Practical and Immediate Tips for Passing Exams

Written by JOB

Cartoons by Ash

The Great Little Book Company Limited Publication

Produced by print**source**uk

Published by The Great Little Book Company Limited

Quantum House PO Box 31, Chichester, West Sussex PO18 8TS

Tel: 01243 572132 Fax: 01243 573151

www.trainthebrain.co.uk

Contents 1

Contents II

Step IV Making Learning Active

Step V Place, Gear & Session

Step VI Memorising & Making Sure

Step VII Showing U Know

How to use this book

- ✓ **Skim** through it; to get an overview
- ✓ **Scan** it again and highlight most important areas to you
- ✓ **Read** through each section in more detail, perhaps noting down key points that will help performance and success rate.
- ✓ **Discuss** your thoughts and findings with others within 24 hours
- ✓ **Focus** on an action plan
- ✓ **Keep an open mind!** (Like a bar - it's best when it's open)

You do not have to have an incredible IQ to pass exams, but you do have to have the ability to revise well.

Why Revise?
Step 1 - Maximise Brain Power

What's the purpose of Exams?

- Different subjects require different skills, these are often called critical thinking skills and they vary from subject to subject.They are all important.
- These skills will be very useful to you in whatever you do later in life.
- To be able to prove you can use these skills without 'props' to hand (like books & resources) is equally important.
  It's the skill (as well as the grade) that's vital.
- You also need to 'Show You Know' how to learn. Learning to Learn is a greatly underestimated skill and one you need everyday of your life!
  You must identify and exploit your own unique style.
- You also need to show the ability to take responsibility for your work; organising, planning and self motivating is a skill others need to recognise in you.
- The ability to Memorise and Problem Solve are equally important too.
- You also need to prove to yourself that you have the willpower and the mindpower.

This pocketbook is re-inforced by The Great Little Book of BrainPower;
Together they can help you make a difference to your life.

Thinking Skills for Life

If you're good at the following skills, you'll be proving, through hard work, your Revision and your Exams that you've met the standard to move on;

Prioritising .... putting knowledge into a sequence of importance
Sorting and classifying .... seeing similarities in different information
Evaluating .... seeing what is important about the information
Transferring .... using the knowledge in different situations
Analysing .... spotting a pattern emerging from information
Predicting .... guessing outcomes from situations
Planning .... using the information in an ordered way
Creating Solutions .... seeing new uses for knowledge
Problem Solving .... finding answers using the information
Communicating .... explaining the information to others
Testing Solutions, ... proving that the information is correct
Criticising .... seeing what is good and bad about a situation
Hypothesising .... ssolution / answer based on a reasoned theory

Train Your Brain!

Knowing Your Brain is essential because the way your brain is wired will effect how you revise. You can make it better and faster!

You have 3 brains:

They all have different jobs - but to work 3 times faster they have to work together.

- The largest is your Higher Thinking Brain. (HTB)
- The Middle Brain is where your emotions and Long Term Memory are housed.
- The Reptillian deals with basic functions such as safety and security, heart rate, BP and so on

The "HTB" - It has two 'halves'. Each has differing skills.

You will be dominant in one side. Tick those skills that match you.

Which is your strongest?

Left:
Language
Numbers
Logic
Sequence
Linearity
Words
Some Meaning/Imagination

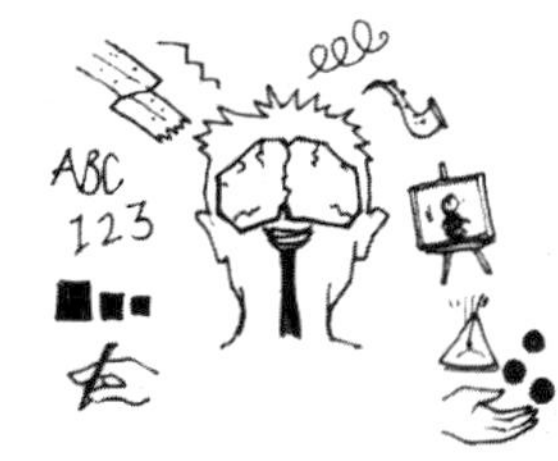

Right:
Colour
Shape/pattern
Music/Rhythm
Experience/Imagination
Meaning
Tunes
Some Language + Maths

Whole Brain Skills

Now you know your dominant half. It would be useful to know WHY it helps!

- Use only one 'half' when learning & you learn at about 35% efficiency.
- Use both at once (combining skills from left & right sides) means you will learn at over 80% efficiency each session!

Benefits

- You build very strong brain cell connections across your brain 3 times faster thinking.
- You remember much faster & easier.
- You save loads of time!!

See Page 48 & 49 for a topic and an example.

Multi-Intelligencies

You also have to learn MANY intelligences fast ....
it's not about maths and languages alone.
If you know your strongest and use them when revising,
you will learn x3 times faster!

	RANK
1. **Linguistic** (Languages) - Reading, Writing, Talking	______
2. **Logical** / Mathematical - Numbers	______
3. **Visual** Spatial - 3D, Shape, Space	______
4. **Musical** - Rhythm, Beat, Rhyme	______
5. **Physical** - Practical, "Hands -on"	______
6. **Interpersonal** - People Skills, Communicating	______
7. **Intrapersonal** -Self Talk, Analysis	______
8. **Creative** - Imagination/Discovery/Ideas	______
9. **Intuitive** - Interpreting and analysing what isn't available to the normal senses	______

Rank your intelligences 1-10 - 1 is the highest

See page 84 for an example of how to use all your intelligences!

How to increase your Memory in half the time!
Smart Reviewing!

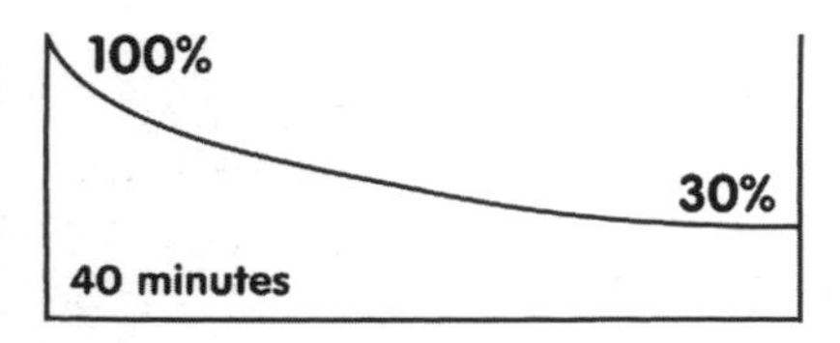

Within 24 hours we forget
70% of what we learn.
So you will have to learn fully,
time and time again.
(Perhaps up to 3 hours on one topic!)

UNLESS ...

We 'review' visual images and lists of facts for a few minutes **twice** within **24** hours, and then regularly every few weeks

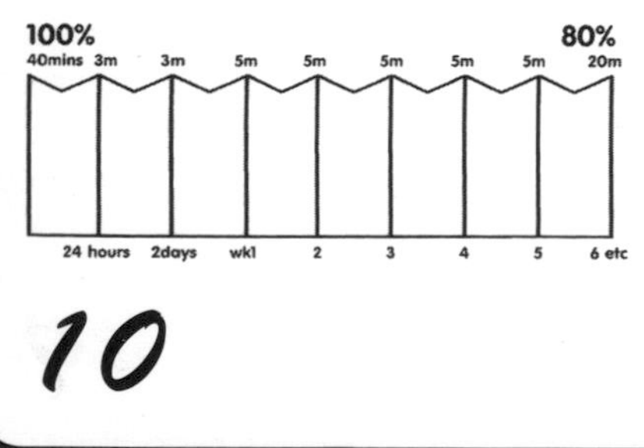

As you draw closer to the exams
you will probably need
some longer sessions.

Which do you prefer -
90 minutes or 3 hours?

How Multi-Skills Help You Learn & Remember
Multi-Brain & Intelligence Skills
Higher Brain
Remember
VISUAL
AUDITORY
PRACTICAL
Information taken in through ALL Senses to SHORT TERM MEMORY
Information to be repeated and revised twice in 24 hours before it enters your LONG TERM MEMORY
Information not reinforced falls out of memory (70% within 24 hours)
11

Sensational Learning

As you can tell from the diagram on page 11 if you learn using all your senses, both 'sides' of your brain and all your intelligences, your Learning & Memory increase by three times, and it doesn't take you so long!

Assess your Strongest Learning Channel

Revising By **Listening**
("Sounds good to me")
Talkers.
Listens but impatient to talk.
Prefer to be told than shown.
Talk to themselves.
Listening to radio / music important.
Untidy
Prefer Listening lessons.

Revision Skills
Read out loud.
Discuss and teach.
Tape info.
Hear their own "voice"
memory like reading aloud.
Tell other your diary plans.

TICK THOSE THAT MATCH YOU ✓

Revising by **'Seeing'**

("I can see what you mean")
Prefer meeting and seeing videos, diagrams, reading.
Poor Listeners.
Like maps not oral directions.
Doodle.
Gives visual presentations
Tidy

Revision Skills:

Patterned Notes.
Visualise in the head.
Draw pictures / illustrations.
Use visual memory aids.
Use film, video, posters, colour
Use visual diaries.

Revising by **'Doing / Feeling'**

Prefers "hands on",
"Hang on!" tactile
Relax through activity (hobby / sport)
Prefer to "do and talk"
Fidget, don't like sitting still
Use gestures & expressions

Making models.
Copying information while listening.
Like active visual notes
Move while learning.
Underline. Hi-light

TICK THOSE THAT MATCH YOU ✓

YOUR REVISION PERSONALITY
Are you a Skydiver?

(who likes the 'big picture' - an overview of everything?)

- ❑ sees new & other ways of doing things
- ❑ sees the total picture
- ❑ uses lots of resources at once
- ❑ likes variety and excitement
- ❑ becomes totally involved in interesting topics
- ❑ tries new ideas and creative techniques
- ❑ visualises & imagines well

- ❑ can forget important details
- ❑ can be disorganised & easily distracted
- ❑ delays before starting
- ❑ doesn't stick to plans
- ❑ only works in bursts - often at the last moment
- ❑ forgets resources (e.g. books)
- ❑ doesn't file or rework notes
- ❑ doesn't plan or stick to plans when made
- ❑ rushes into answers without thinking

Or are you an Intrepid Explorer?

(who likes to work step by step through a project or topic)

- ❑ organises facts and materials well
- ❑ sees links between ideas
- ❑ enjoys problems and their solutions
- ❑ is precise, thorough and meticulous
- ❑ plans everyday work and revision well
- ❑ reworks notes and essay plans
- ❑ isn't easily distracted
- ❑ reads instructions carefully
- ❑ researches exam syllabus thoroughly
- ❑ likes to understand every aspect of a topic

- ❑ needs too much information before starting work
- ❑ doesn't consult teachers or others enough
- ❑ won't try new approaches
- ❑ can be set in his/her ways
- ❑ sees only one way of doing something
- ❑ is often preoccupied with details

You need to be a bit of both! To know your preference will help you plan how you study a subject or topic. Which is your strongest?

If you know your strengths and weaknesses from each personality - then you will know what you have to achieve. These can become targets for success.

Which is your 'stronger' personality?______________________________

Memory & Forgetting

When you sit down to revise you must concentrate on what stops you forgetting as well as clever memory tricks & techniques.

- You can't learn anything properly, unless you understand it.
- You must have excellent listening skills
- You must review work regularly and review it again within 24 hours of a long session

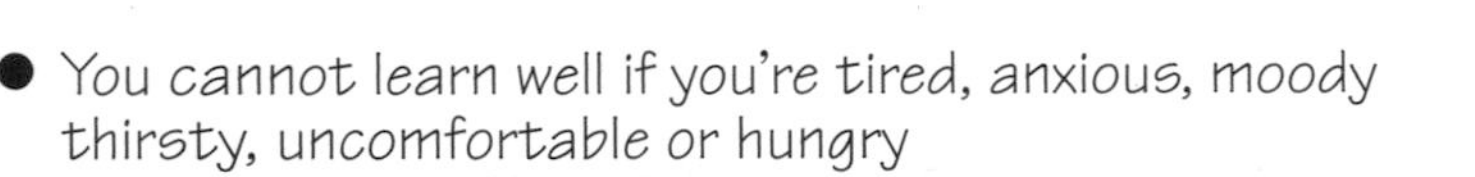

- You cannot learn well if you're tired, anxious, moody thirsty, uncomfortable or hungry
- You cannot learn well without sorting the work into categories

If you allow any form of interruption or distraction, learning can take you three times longer!

Concentration and Time

We know that you concentrate best for about 40 minutes at a time. Any longer and concentration lapses - learning is ineffective & takes you longer

This chart shows you why 30-40 mins is a good length of concentration time.

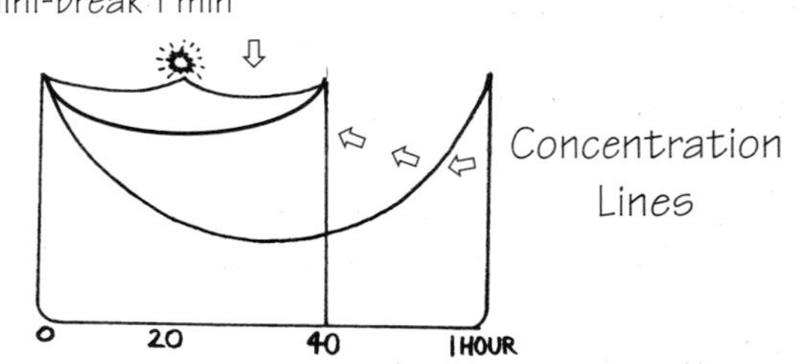

- If you revise for an hour your "low concentration" time is greater. It's better to revise for 35-40 minutes with 5-10 minute breaks in between.
- Learning is best in the morning when your 'subconcious' mind is less cluttered.
- Once you have worked on a topic it is essential to review it twice for a few minutes within 24 hours.

SUMMARY

To Revise Well you need to Train Your Brain

KNOW YOUR BRAIN!

TOP 3 **INTELLIGENCES?**

1

2

3

Which helps you revise best?

....

....

....

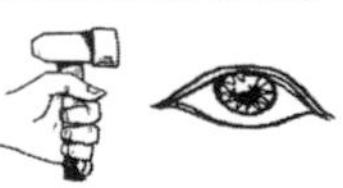

R or L Brain Stronger?

....

Your Learning

Personality . . . Skydiver? ☐

Explorer? ☐

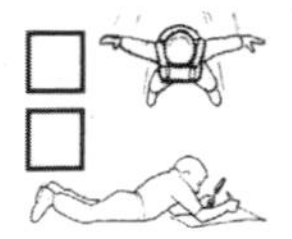

What can you improve?

1

2

3

What is your strongest

Sense? (VAP)

See 1.......................................

Do 2.......................................

Say/Hear 3.......................................

Step 2 - Mind Power for Revising

"If students paid more attention to looking after their mind - they would almost certainly double results in half the time!"

This chapter includes:

- Positive Thinking and Fast Learning
- Motivation, Determination & Commitment
- Concentration and Attention Span
- Inspiration
- Managing Pressure

It is control of the following that makes the difference:

Positive v Negative...
...the facts

There is no doubt that learning takes place much faster if you can control your positive state of mind.

Try to:

- See a difficult task as a challenge not a threat.
- See opportunities not problems.
- Consider that all ideas and suggestions are possible.
- Avoid negative and damaging 'moaners'.
- See 'failure' as temporary.
- Speak and act positively and enthusiastically.
- Use positive gestures: smile often, have a cheerful tone of voice.
- Look forwards not back.

Did You Know:

- A positive approach enables 3 times faster learning.
- You become more negative as you tire - so work earlier in the day.
- You will be more positive if you find a purpose.
- Share your thoughts / concerns with a positive supporter.

Motivation

Motivation is a positive force to help you achieve your aim - if planned and applied it **changes behaviour** and breaks through negative mindsets.

The good news is that it is possible to motivate yourself.... even to revise!

If your idea of revision is to stare endlessly at your work hoping to 'beam it up' or take detailed copies of your notes word for word... then it's not surprising you're not wild about it and therefore it's hard to get on with it.

Hopefully this little book will show you how to really train your brain and so motivate you to determined effort... but the following steps will help

- Look to the future - what sort of life do you want? Create your 'Success Dream'.
- Look for the purpose in your studies; 'If I do this, I will be able to...'
- Take pride in your work performance. record all successes.
- Look back at previous success. Remember how you felt then.

Motivation continued

- Plan your work into a timetable - month, week and day. Set **'Smart Targets' (p31)**.
- Use a time planner to help see the big picture. Plan in your free time activities.
- Break your topics down into manageable chunks.
- Set sensible time limits; it's not the number of hours you put in, it's what you put into them.
- Talk to someone who knows what you're going through. (Your 'learning supporter'.) Any praise and understanding from them will motivate you.
- Avoid comparisons with others
- Praise yourself when you know you've got it right! Give yourself a reward!
- Develop a mental vision of yourself succeeding.

Try them! You'll be surprised!

Relaxation, Concentration & Your α Brain Waves!

Research has clearly shown that brain activity increases and learning is faster if you can create a 'Mindstate' that encourages Alpha brain waves in your LTM. This is a state when you are relaxed yet focused. Your normal conscious learning involves 'beta' brain waves in your STM. Using both brain waves creates a massive gateway to your memory.

How to increase brain waves for fast learning:

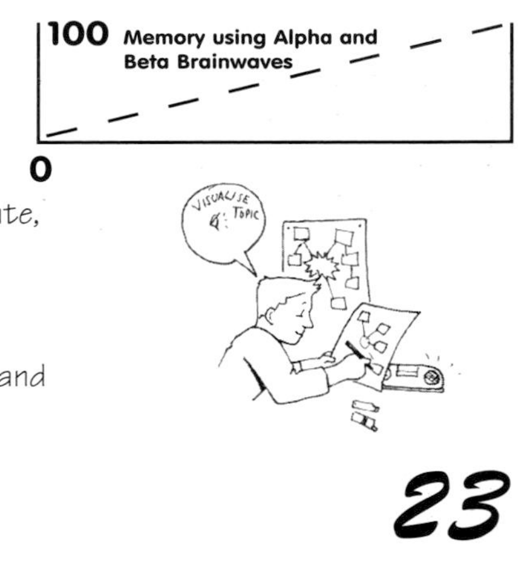

- Work in quiet comfortable surrounding.
- Play non-lyrical music at about 60 beats a minute, in line with your heartbeat.
- Use multi-sensory activities; see page 72.
- Learn to 'Visualise' a topic.
- Start with simple tasks - colouring / shading in and around notes (Brain frames).

Creating a Focused Mood
(continued)

- Do something ambi-dexterous like doodling with both hands or juggling. (Links all parts of your brain!) for these "snap" concentration.
- Put up posters or diagrams ... you learn 'subliminally'.
- Don't eat heavily just before sitting down to work. Avoid foods that have chemical additives (such as crisps, fizzy drinks or wine gums!)
- Don't set yourself too much to do (or too little!).
- Don't work for more than 35-40 minutes before mini-breaks (5-10mins).
- Work in the mornings when your mind is not cluttered with other things.
- Don't try 'new' learning at night or when tired.
- Drink water occasionally - avoid feeling thirsty. Don't try to drink too much at once. (about 2 litres a day, sipped regularly).
- Build in rewards and new ways to relax.

Finding the Inspiration and Peak Performance

You will need to:

- Create Alpha Brain State (see pages 23 and 24).
- Visualise a past success, daydream a future success (it doesn't have to be academic).
- If you feel negative - use bottom-line thinking. Imagine the worst possible situation and list ways of avoiding it.
- Drink some water; have a brain booster. (Small amount of chocolate or peppermint).
- Make sure you are comfortable. Sitting - keep your spine straight.
- Create a challenge.
- Lay out your area so you know where everything is.
- Link your 'brains' through ambidextrous activity.
- Try a few lateral thinking exercises (often called brain teasers).
- Brainstorm ideas (as many as possible and as crazy as you want!).
- Write them down, spread over a blank page.

This all takes practice but definitely helps creativity.

Dealing With Pressure

We all experience pressure - sometimes this can become stressful and this results in various reactions from feeling physically ill (headache, tummy ache etc.) or fed up (worried, fearing the worst, anxious.) We all worry about 'Revision' but often a more accurate reason is on the list below:

What stresses one person need not stress another.

Cause of Stress:

Illness	Putting things off until the last minute
Being unfit	Negative thinking
A poor diet	Work mounting up
Low energy	Incompetence or imagined incompetence
People being annoying or demanding	Interruptions, Distractions
No praise / support	Trying to do too much at once
Targets that are unrealistic and therefore not hit!	Not understanding work
	Not knowing your learning style

Tick any that have stressed you.

Remedies for Stress

Firstly recognise you're stressed. The try some or all of these:

- Exercise - get moving!
- Seek advice
- Control your time
- Plan in rewards, fun & relaxation
- Work in 'chunks' not 'wholes'
- Relaxation techniques such as: tensing and then relaxing your muscles, stretching and unwinding moving up from feet to face
- Balance your diet and eat sensibly
- Try Yoga or Massage
- Laughter releases endorphins (the body's painkillers) and they allow more energy.
- Try to predict the difficult times
- Get enough sleep and rest
- Talk positively to yourself
- Plan your goals and dream them!
- Create a manageable daily routine
- Act happy!
- Talk to people who are positive and reassuring and see your friends
- Don't vegitate - do something worthwhile
- Stand back from the problem and try to see it from another angle

F: Fitness
R: Relaxation
E: Energy
D: Diet
S: Sleep

And take control of your FREDS

The Power of Imagination

It is probably your most powerful thinking skill

Imagination means using thought pictures.

It is about using information or knowledge you already know and seeing it in another situation as well as inventing new ideas and creating images or pictures of them in your head.

There was a football coach who carried out a survey of his players. He asked some to practise their penalties every day for 14 days, a second group to stop practising altogether, and a third group practise on the first and last days and imagine their penalties and success for 40 minutes each day.

After two weeks the first group showed 40% improvement, the second group - 0% improvement.......and the third group - also 40% improvement!

So what would they have achieved if they had practised a lot and used their imagination also to learn? Try this with your Revision!

A positive imagination will enable you to learn

3 times FASTER AND BETTER!

Have a go!

Working with Others

Many students revise in pairs or groups. Testing each other helps, but teaching each other is more beneficial. Be careful who you choose - some groups have 'saboteurs'. Involve everyone, assign tasks if possible and encourage constructively. Watch for those who copy rather than contribute. You can use your multi intelligences.

THERE ARE MANY BENEFITS

- More Fun
- Saves time
- More brains - different styles
- Individuals try harder for the group
- Mutual support
- Greater creativity

- More creative
- Often faster
- NB: Find a 'Learning Supporter' for reassurance, advice and ideas!

And then you're a group 'saviour'.

Visualisation

Try closing your eyes and running a 'mental movie' in your head. Imagine seeing, feeling & hearing your success in any exam. Look at the images on this page to help you gain this visual image. Use your visual spacial intelligence.

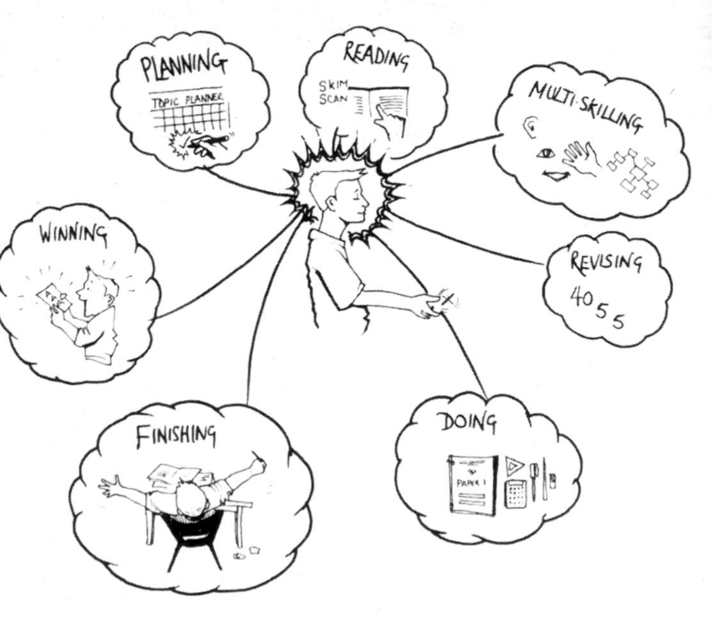

Step 3 - Time Control

Once you have a good idea of the Timescale and what you have to do, the whole Revision processed is eased.
Good time planning is one of the most important skills you need.
And it's not that difficult to manage.....
This section will help you do it!

- Targets and Dreams
- Time Planning
- Time Management
- Revision Plans & Timetables
- Reviewing Your Learning

Take the Long View

It's much easier to sit down to work, especially when temptations are tugging at your motivation and concentration, when you have a long term vision or dream.

- *Look beyond the exams. What do you want to do?* ____________________

- *What have you to look forward to?* ____________________

- *What do you want to achieve?* ____________________

- *Begin to set targets and daydream your future.*

It sounds simple... it is - and it works

Manage Your Time

Analyse How You Spend Your Time - you have 168 hours in the week.

- How long do you spend working on compulsory activities?
- How long do you spend looking after yourself? (sleeping, eating etc. - maintaining yourself)
- Subtract this total of hours from 168 and you are left with the number of hours that are your FREE hours.
- Could you make better use of your own time? Yes/No
  Are you wasting it? ....
  What wastes it? ....

- Keep a record of your normal week: you'll soon see where the time goes.

Working=		168
Maintaining=		
	-	
TOTAL Free Time=	+	

What's wasting / using up your time? ______________________________

____

____

How could you save time?______________________________________

____

Look at the Year Ahead

You should have a constant clear view.

What are your deadlines:-

In six months?

In a month?

Next week?

Depend on a Time Planner

Use an Organiser (A Time Planning System) and you'll:

- Having a clear 'map' of your year, month, week and day places you in greater control.
- You can predict the tough times and plan in your enjoyment! You will feel re-assured that you will leave 'no stone unturned.'

Planners and Personal Organisers have many other abilities - note pads, financial pages, project / assignment planners, address and contacts pages and many more.
You can also plan your goals for the year, targets to help meet the deadlines and your weekly / daily tasks,
so that you feel in control of your life.
You can also plan in things you enjoy and don't want to miss.

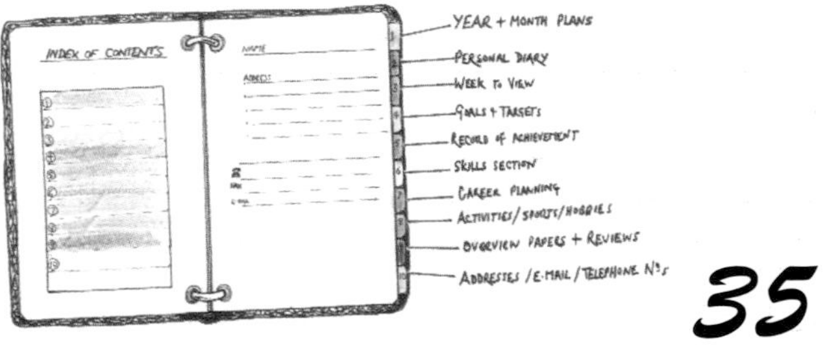

Prioritise and List Your Tasks

✓ It is good practice to list all your tasks, academic and personal on a weekly and daily basis.

✓ Once listed, you can put them in a priority order of immediate importance.

- A priorities, B priorities, and C priorities.
- And prioritise them further B^1, B^2 etc. if necessary.
- You can now plan them into your day and week
- It will allow you to complete C priorities as well as A's and B's. This is often good for motivation and enjoyment!

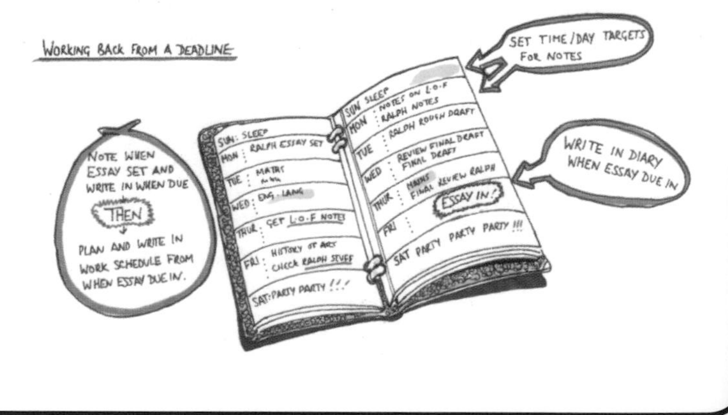

SMARTEST - Set daily Targets / Tasks

S	specific	- Know exactly what's wanted.
M	measurable	- Be able to assess how you've done.
A	attainable	- You must understand it and know you can achieve it.
R	realistic	- i.e Don't try to do too much or set ridiculous targets
T	timed	- in 30-40 mini chunks; learn to 'guesstimate' how long it will take you.
E	evaluate	- Assess how you've done
S	success	- How does this help your overall success plan?
T	targetted	- Once one target is achieved look to the next

Why is Setting Targets Good For You?

✓ You remain in control of your time and, when planned sensibly, this can be both flexible and rewarding so you can do all you have to do and want to do.

✓ Segment studying is very important for memory, motivation and success - break down you work into manageable chunks.

✓ Work back from your deadline:

Ask yourself questions:-

How long will take me to write, draft & check? How many drafts?

How long will it take me to select information? How long will it take me to plan it?

How long will it take to interpret the question / problem and to initially brainstorm?

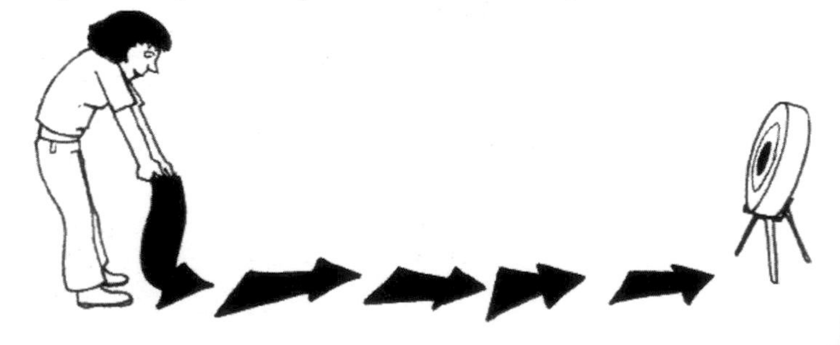

Topic Lists and Overview "Brainframes"

For each topic of any reasonable size you should create a topic "Overview Template".

It can be any pattern - Brainmap, Wheel pattern (as below), flow chart, spray notes.... vary it from topic to topic. These are Brainframes. (See pages 47-64).

Don't add any detail yet. Just create a 2 minute template!

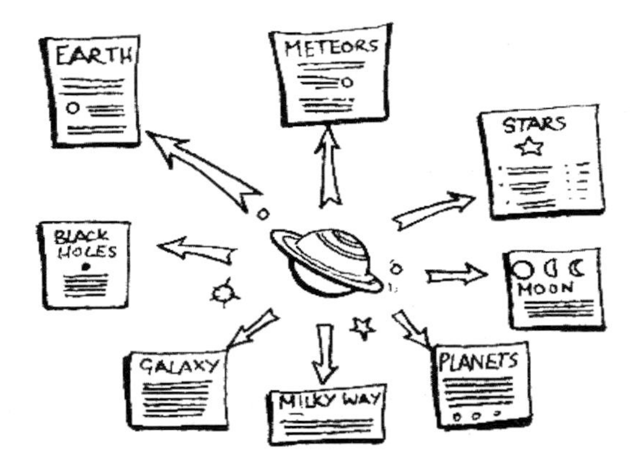

Topic Assessment and Reviews

- Ask your teacher for lists of topics.
- Break them into manageable chunks (i.e. what you can revise in c.40 mins).
- Go through the list and estimate how well you know it (give it a % for example - I know this 10%, 50%, 90% etc.).
- Now estimate how many minutes you think it will take you (i.e. 40 mins).
- Then add 1/3 more time... it always takes longer than you think!!

Subject: Biology
Section One - Plants

Revision Sessions — Syllabus Review Chart

				24hrs		1wk	2wks	4wks	8wks		12wks etc.		
Topic	40	40	40	1	2	3	4	5	6	7	8	9	10
Life Processes and cells 50% (1 HR)	✓			✓	✓								
Specialised Plant Cells 40% (90 mins)	✓	✓		✓	✓	✓	✓						
Diffusion 30% (130 mins)													
Diffusion Through Cell Membranes 30 %													
Osmosis 90% (20 mins)	✓			✓	✓	✓	✓	✓					
Basic Plant Structure 40% (90 mins)													
Leaf Structure 75% (30 mins)													

Allow 2-5 mins each for Reviews

Working with your Syllabus Topics

- As you go through each topic, tick it off.
- Review your topic for 2 mins twice in 24 hours. (Best just before and after sleep!).

Tick Reviews off on your list.

- It will also help to plan when you want to complete topics or review them in a long term monthly calendar.

MONTHLY CALENDAR

MON	TUE	WED	THU	FRI	SAT	SUN
1	2	3	4	5	6	7
8	9	10	11	12	13	14
15	16	17	18	19	20	21
22	23	24	25	26	27	28
29	30	31				

This is your general **Revision Timetable** & all topics should be on it.

The Revision Session

40 minute concentration - Tips on how to run a session:

5 mins:	Collect Info / data / resources. Check what you really need to learn.
5 mins:	Overview topic... bring it to the front of your mind.
20-25 mins:	Multi-Sensory Revision (notes, tape, maps, teach 'n test, past paper)
5 mins:	Assess what you've learnt. What needs more attention? Mark on your overview Brainframe.

"When is it best to revise?"

Early in the day for 'New' learning
- initial topic revision.
Late afternoon for an extra topic or two
Evening - 5 min reviews of what you've done
Morning - Review them again first thing next day

Revising on top of a busy schedule

(During term time)

It's always difficult to start any Revision Learning when you're still working at normal pace and a normal timetable.

- Try to fit in time to set up Topic Lists and Overview Sheets.
- Review topics at night.
- Try to give up some time at weekends for especially difficult topics

Full Time Revision

Routine is vital.

- Make a weekly timetable. Check your monthly calendar. Make sure your weekly TT matches it!
- Work in the mornings. Start with a review of Topics from yesterday.

i.e 9.30 - 10.10	**Topic 1 (+break)**
10.15 - 10.55	**Topic 2 (+break)**
11.00 - 11.40	**Topic 3**
11.40 - 12.00	**Break**
2.00 - 12.40	**Topic 4**
Lunch	
1.40 - 3.40	**Free / Break / Friends / Excercise etc.**
3.40 - 4.20	**Topic 5**

- Evenings; Review 5 Topics for 5 mins using (c.9.00 pm) Use your overview Brainframes (25 mins)

Save Time! Collect Equipment & Resources in Advance

Time spent chasing equipment becomes frustrating.
Equipment falls into various categories:

- Tools (pen, paper, colours etc.)
- Filing - boxes, index, systems, files, folders.
- Resources (notes, texts, journals, newspapers and articles etc.)
- Equipment - audio tape, lamp, printer, chair, large desk.

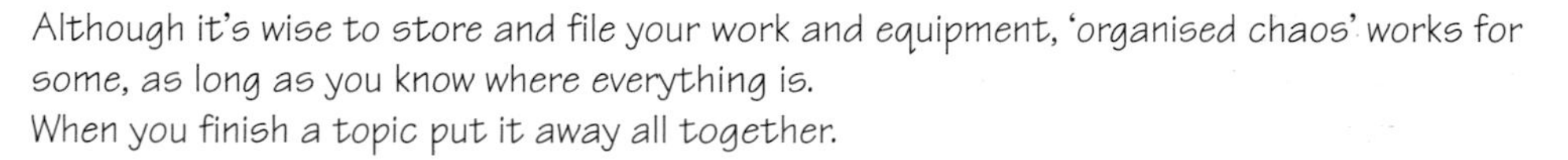

Although it's wise to store and file your work and equipment, 'organised chaos' works for some, as long as you know where everything is.
When you finish a topic put it away all together.

Have supplies and rewards

H_2O - water regularly taken helps concentration and faster thinking.
An energy booster (i.e a small amount of chocolate) is also important.
Work towards something you like for each part of your day, these are motivational rewards.

Learn to Read to Save Time

You don't need to read every word of your revision resource material (notes, texts, articles etc.) Unnecessary or insufficient reading often wastes time. Effective reading is not about speed but about understanding and comprehension. Ask Yourself your purpose and need.

- Learn to **Skim** (let your eyes move fast through the text to gauge the value and relevance).
  Look at the contents, the index, the concluding chapter and opening and concluding paragraphs.
- Learn to **Scan**. Look for key ideas, names, phrases, illustrations, quotes and data by scanning across the page, let your eyes zig zag as you go. Read the first and last paragraph sentences.
- Learn to read in detail - **Scour!** Use the punctuation and guide (ruler / finger).
  Try to avoid backtracking (when you re-read sentences or your mind wanders).
  Set minutes for your reading: not hours or moments. Use adequate lighting, avoid reflective surfaces and keep a distance of about 30 cms /18 inches.
  - To maintain concentration - take 2-5 minute breaks every 15 minutes.
  - Relax after an hour.

Step 4 - Making Learning Active - Brain Framer

The key to really knowing a topic is to use your WHOLE BRAIN! - We introduce here the easiest and fastest method of:

- ◆ Clarifying
- ◆ Understanding
- ◆ Memorising
- ◆ Building Knowledge
- ◆ Remembering
- ◆ Planning & Answering in Exams

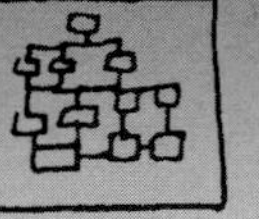

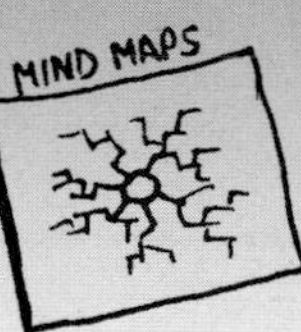

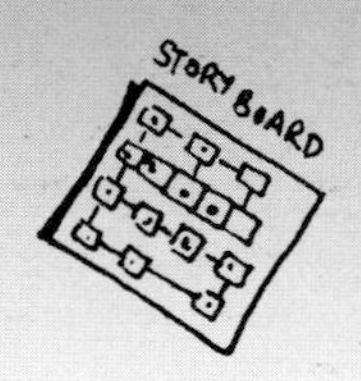

- You need an OVERVIEW / REVIEW sheet.
- You need LISTS of facts / data (Left Brain).
- You need to add detail from time to time. You need pattern, shape, colour, the whole picture and individual unique pages. (Right Brain)
- You need VISUALISATION - to help you remember and plan answers. (Right Brain)

You need BRAIN FRAMES! In Four or more Phases I, II, III, IV.

Why it Works & Why It's Crucial to Your Success

Brain framer has proved enourmously successful to all ages because:

- They're Easy
- You can be built upon, layer by layer, phase by phase.
- You can add to them
- You can design them for yourself
- You can see obvious connections, choose order/sequence
- You can use them for any subject
- They replicate your "whole" brain

There are many types of NOTE TAKING from the very 'left hemisphere' linear list to the very 'right hemisphere' mind maps. Brain frames make the most of both styles.

How to Create Brain Frame Revision Notes

Phase I → Create a Simple Topic Overview
Main Headings & Bullet Points (blank)

Plate Boundaries:

-
-
-
-

Earthquakes

Constructive

-
-
-

Destructive

-
-
-

Conservative/Transform

-
-
-
-

MAGMA

FAULTS

PLATE

PLATE

Leave other side of sheet blank

Time taken -
5 mins -
It doesn't have to be perfect

→ Add key facts to bullet points (in pencil)

Draw diagrams (clear not perfect)

Plate Boundaries:

- Unstable Areas = Often Volcanic / Earthquake Zones
- Nazca Plate
- N/a Plate - Pacific Plate
- San Andreas Fault

Earthquakes

Constructive

- Pulling Apart
- Causes New Crust
- Therefore Ridges, Rift Valleys, Volcanic Islands, i.e N/a & Eurasion Plates meet

MAGMA

FAULTS

Destructive

- Colliding plates
- Crusts subduct & collapse / meet
- Therefore Fold Mountain or ocean trough, i.e Nazca & South American

PLATE

PLATE

Conservative/Transform

- Sliding along each other
- = Friction therefore no crust
- i.e San Andreas Fault (Pacific and North American plates)

Time taken - 30 mins - It doesn't have to be perfect

→ Replace pencilled key / vital words with bright ink
Replace rest of pencilled with normal black/blue.
Print some words if possible.
Add extra if necessary
Shade each area

Plate Boundaries:

- **Unstable** Areas = Often Volcanic / Earthquake Zones
- **Nazca** Plate
- **N/A Plate** - Pacific Plate
- **San Andreas** Fault

Constructive

- **Pulling** Apart
- Causes **New Crust**
- Therefore Ridges, Rift Valleys, Volcanic Islands, i.e N/a & Eurasion Plates meet

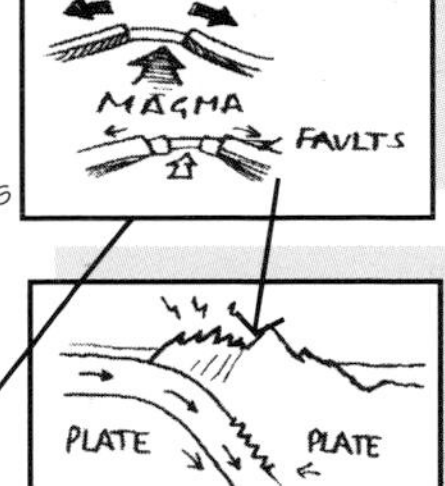

Destructive

- **Colliding** plates
- Crusts **subduct** & collapse / meet
- Therefore Fold Mountain or ocean trough, i.e Nazca & South American

Conservative/Transform

- **Sliding** along each other
- = **Friction** therefore no crust
- i.e San Andreas Fault (Pacific and North American plates)

Time taken
10 mins

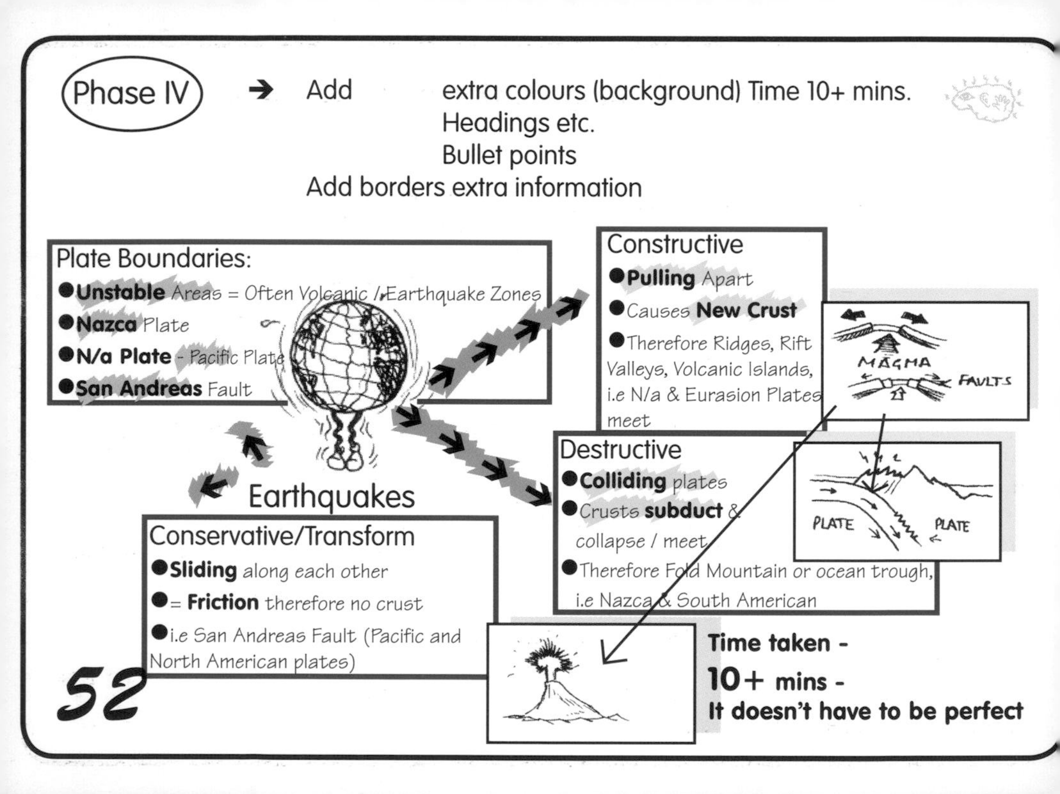

Phase IV
Add extra colours (background) Time 10+ mins.
Headings etc.
Bullet points
Add borders extra information
Plate Boundaries:
Unstable Areas = Often Volcanic / Earthquake Zones
Nazca Plate
N/a Plate - Pacific Plate
San Andreas Fault
Constructive
Pulling Apart
Causes New Crust
Therefore Ridges, Rift Valleys, Volcanic Islands, i.e N/a & Eurasion Plates meet
MAGMA
FAULTS
Destructive
Colliding plates
Crusts subduct & collapse / meet
Therefore Fold Mountain or ocean trough, i.e Nazca & South American
PLATE
PLATE
Earthquakes
Conservative/Transform
Sliding along each other
= Friction therefore no crust
i.e San Andreas Fault (Pacific and North American plates)
Time taken -
10+ mins -
It doesn't have to be perfect

An example of Modern History GCSE Topic

LEAGUE of NATIONS

Why & when established:
- After WW1
- To stop war
- To end large group coalitions

Reason for Being/Purpose:
- To bring humanitarian aid
- Peace Keeping force
- To bring international justice
- To impose sanctions

STRUCTURE

ASSEMBLEY

Court of International Justice

Council

Secretariat

ILO

Agencies

Mandates

Failures:
- Corfu 1923
- Rhur Valley 1923
- Ethiopia

Successes:
- 1921 Aaland Islands
- 1925 Greece v Bulgaria
- 1921 Upper Silesia
- 1923 Menel

Reasons for Failure:
- No Army
- Indecision
- No US/Russian Support
- Selfish aims of individual countries (Franco/British)

Assembly=
Council=
Secretariat=
Agencies: International labour organisation..... Health....... Drugs......
Leprosy..... Refugees..... Slavery.....

A Level Science

CONDUCTION

DEFINITION: Transfer of energy through an objects. ATOMS changing position.

DESCRIPTION: Particles at lower end of rod = energy from the fire = vibration
Extra movement has 'knock on' effect & disturbs/vibrates move particles. They become WARM.
Travels whole length All warm. Energy 'conducted' along it all.

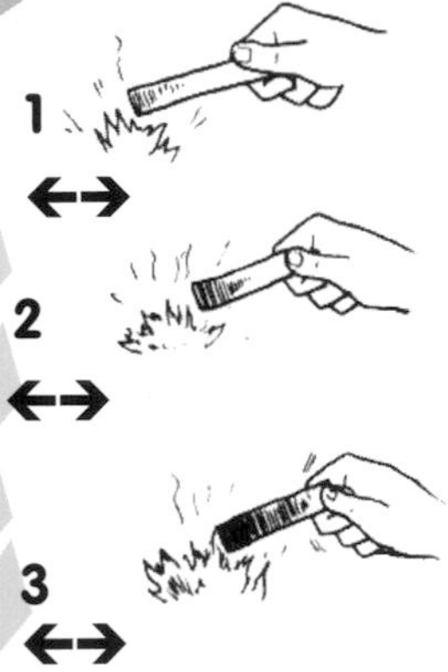

1 ↔

2 ↔

3 ↔

Metals = good conductors
Wood /plastics /ceramics = poor
Some materials restrict heat transfer (INSULATORS)
i.e Cork coaster i.e Paper wrapped around half metal / wood bar ...
When heated paper on wood burns.
BUT paper on metal.

Why? Metal allows heat to pass through paper & escape therefore it doesn't burn. It is a good conductor... wood / paper burns = poor conductor.

A Level Business - Studies/ GNVQ

MASLOW ON MOTIVATION

Definition Motivation: 'A force of process which impels people to behave in the way they do'? Is their behaviour consistent to the organisation's aims? Psychologists have spent much time on this.

Ability.v.Motivation: Differences in results not just M but also ABILITY (check @ interview)

1	2	3	4	5
Psychological Food Water = Pay Sex Holiday Rest	**Safety** Stability NO = Pensions / Safe buyer? job	**Social** Love Friendship =Social Belonging Events ??????? Team Work	**Ego-Esteem** Self Respect — Power Titles Promotion Others Respect — Merit Awards	**Self Satisfaction** Self Fulfilment. Highest Potential = Challenges, New Skills, Success

Criticisms of Maslow:

1. Satisfaction = not the only motivator
2. Some people not interested in 4 or 5
3. Some satisfaction met outside work.
4. Creative people may focus on 4+5 even when 1-3 unsettled

Others on Motivation

- McLelland
- McGregor X & Y Theories
- 'Process' Theories
- Heidelberg 2 Factor

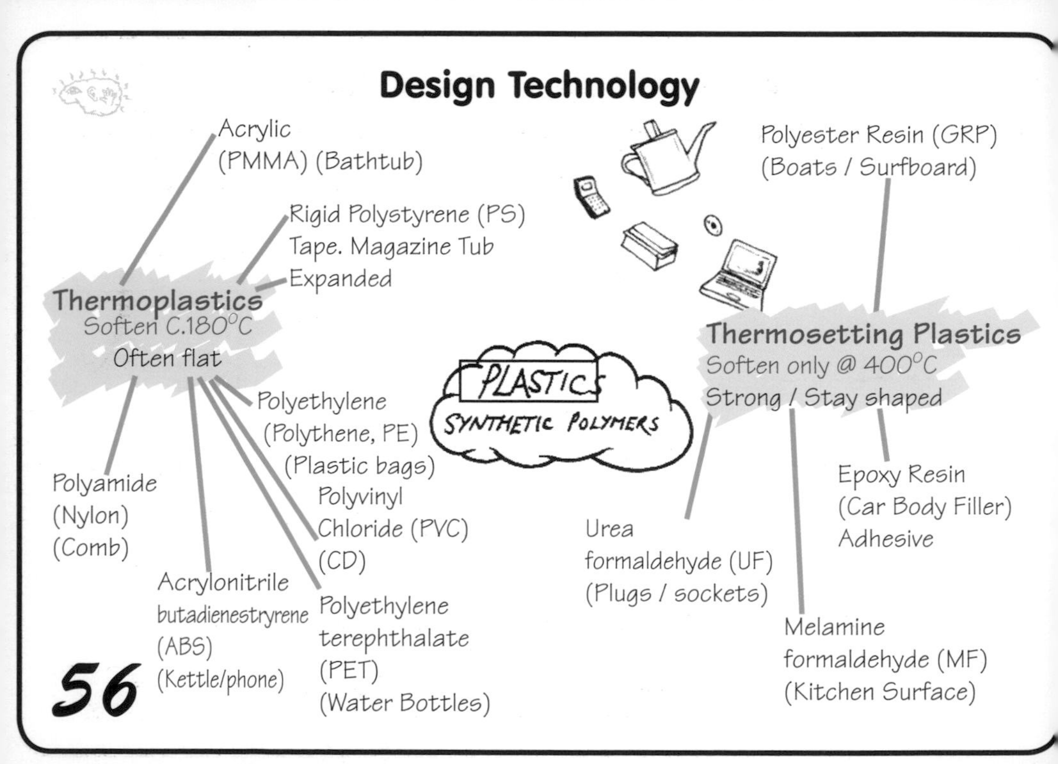
Design Technology
Acrylic
(PMMA) (Bathtub)
Rigid Polystyrene (PS)
Tape. Magazine Tub
Expanded
Polyester Resin (GRP)
(Boats / Surfboard)
Thermoplastics
Soften C.180°C
Often flat
PLASTICS
SYNTHETIC POLYMERS
Thermosetting Plastics
Soften only @ 400°C
Strong / Stay shaped
Polyethylene
(Polythene, PE)
(Plastic bags)
Polyamide
(Nylon)
(Comb)
Polyvinyl
Chloride (PVC)
(CD)
Epoxy Resin
(Car Body Filler)
Adhesive
Urea
formaldehyde (UF)
(Plugs / sockets)
Acrylonitrile
butadienestryrene
(ABS)
(Kettle/phone)
Polyethylene
terephthalate
(PET)
(Water Bottles)
Melamine
formaldehyde (MF)
(Kitchen Surface)
56

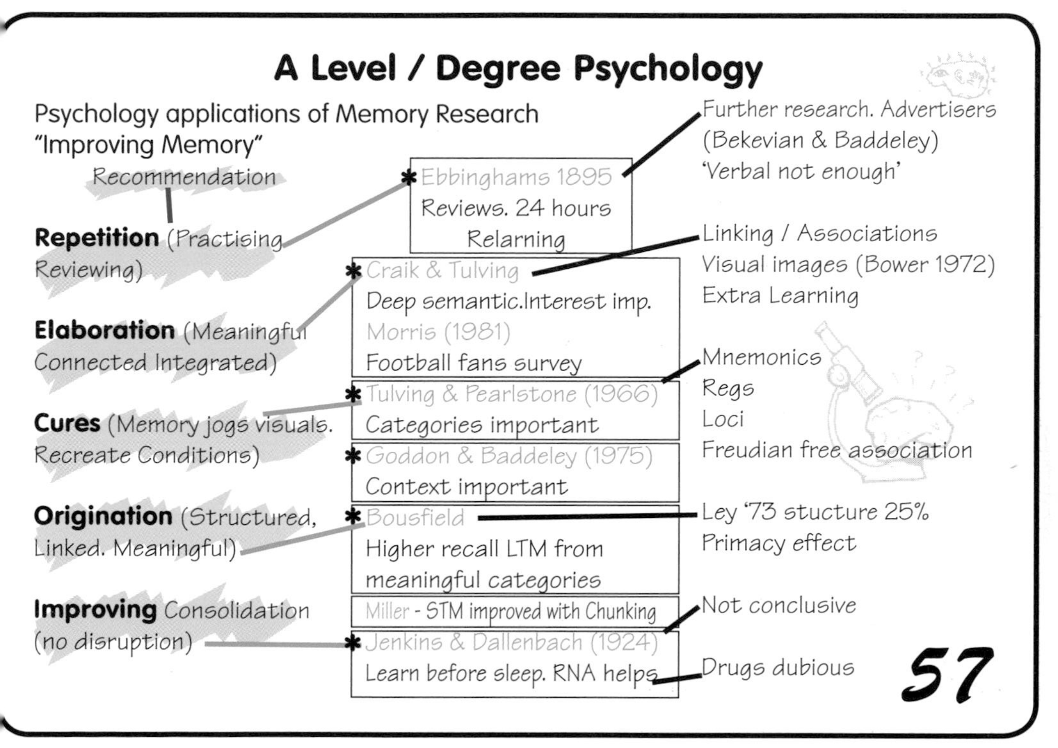
A Level / Degree Psychology
Psychology applications of Memory Research
"Improving Memory"
Recommendation
Repetition (Practising Reviewing)
Elaboration (Meaningful Connected Integrated)
Cures (Memory jogs visuals. Recreate Conditions)
Origination (Structured, Linked. Meaningful)
Improving Consolidation (no disruption)
* Ebbinghams 1895
Reviews. 24 hours
Relarning
* Craik & Tulving
Deep semantic.Interest imp.
Morris (1981)
Football fans survey
* Tulving & Pearlstone (1966)
Categories important
* Goddon & Baddeley (1975)
Context important
* Bousfield
Higher recall LTM from meaningful categories
Miller - STM improved with Chunking
* Jenkins & Dallenbach (1924)
Learn before sleep. RNA helps
Further research. Advertisers
(Bekevian & Baddeley)
'Verbal not enough'
Linking / Associations
Visual images (Bower 1972)
Extra Learning
Mnemonics
Regs
Loci
Freudian free association
Ley '73 stucture 25%
Primacy effect
Not conclusive
Drugs dubious
57

Visualisation

Visual Images are the key to quick remembering.
We've already mentioned visualising your success (see page 29).
Now you should use the following techniques to help you remember your Brainframe Notes & Brainframe Practice Answers:

- *Close your eyes. Relax.*
  Calm regular breathing.
- *Imagine your Brainframe*
  on the back of your eyes.
- *Remember when you drew it.*
- *Say the sub-headings aloud in your head.*
  Recite the lists.
- *Think of your doodles, rhymes, images & charts.*
- *Hold your neurovascular points*
  on your forehead & the back of your neck,
  while you: Visualise the images of your learning

(Also see page 68)

Brain Framer - Adding Extras

NUMBERING AND LETTERING:

i, ii, iii - Main heading
A B C - Sub Heading
1 2 3 - Less important points

SYMBOLS:

@ = approx / about
>< = greater than / lesser than
± = does not equal
◆ Bullet points
◆
◆

COLOURS - Dark Colours (blue/black) for normal notes. Bright colours for key Words. Pastel colours for shading. Highlighters - use sparingly and only when close to the exams.

DIAGRAMS:

Your visual brain must have these. It's not about artistic genius but about understanding and memory.

3D:

DRAWINGS / CARTOONS:

EMPHASIS: Boxes, capitals, bold, highlight, underline, italic.

Past Paper Preparation

On the reverse of each BRAIN FRAME

- Make a list of typical Q's that come up on the topic.
- Map out an imagined Brain Framer plan for an answer

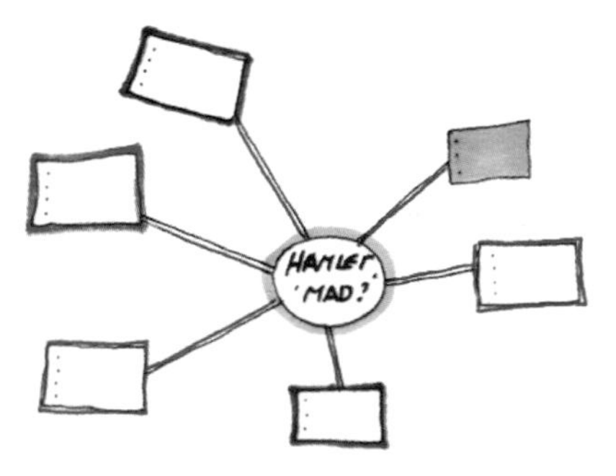

Q1: HAMLET WAS MAD. DISCUSS.
Q2: ROLE OF WOMEN IN HAMLET.

Practice Page

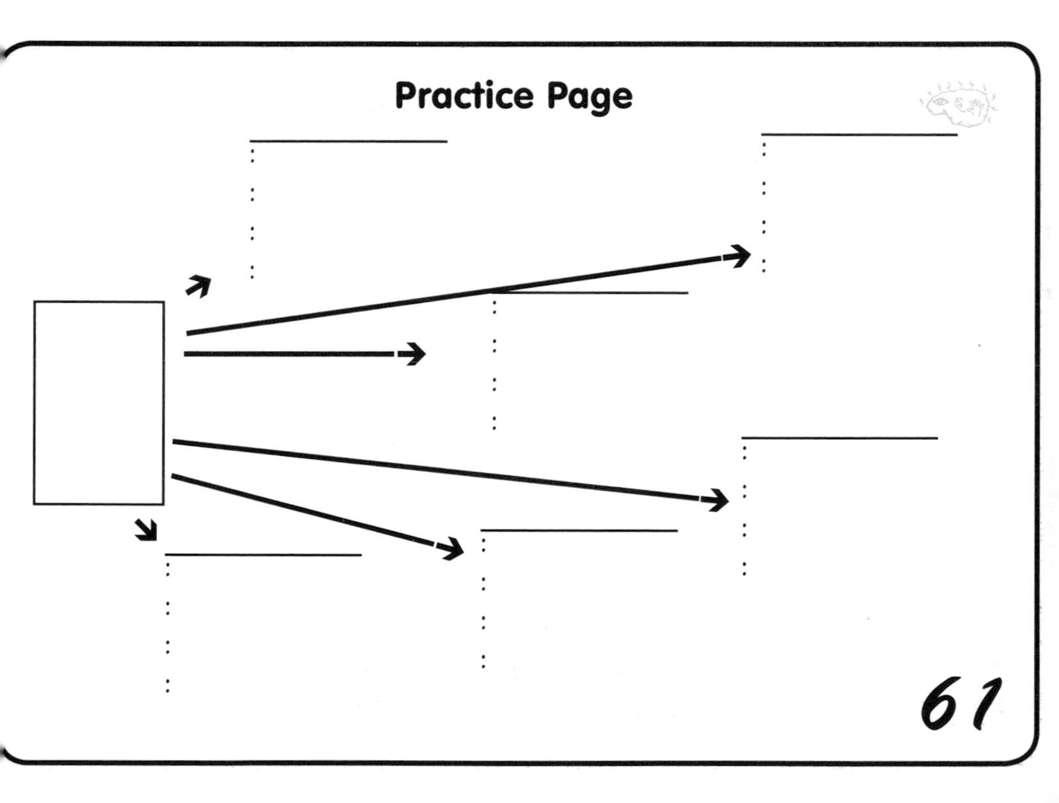

Practice Page

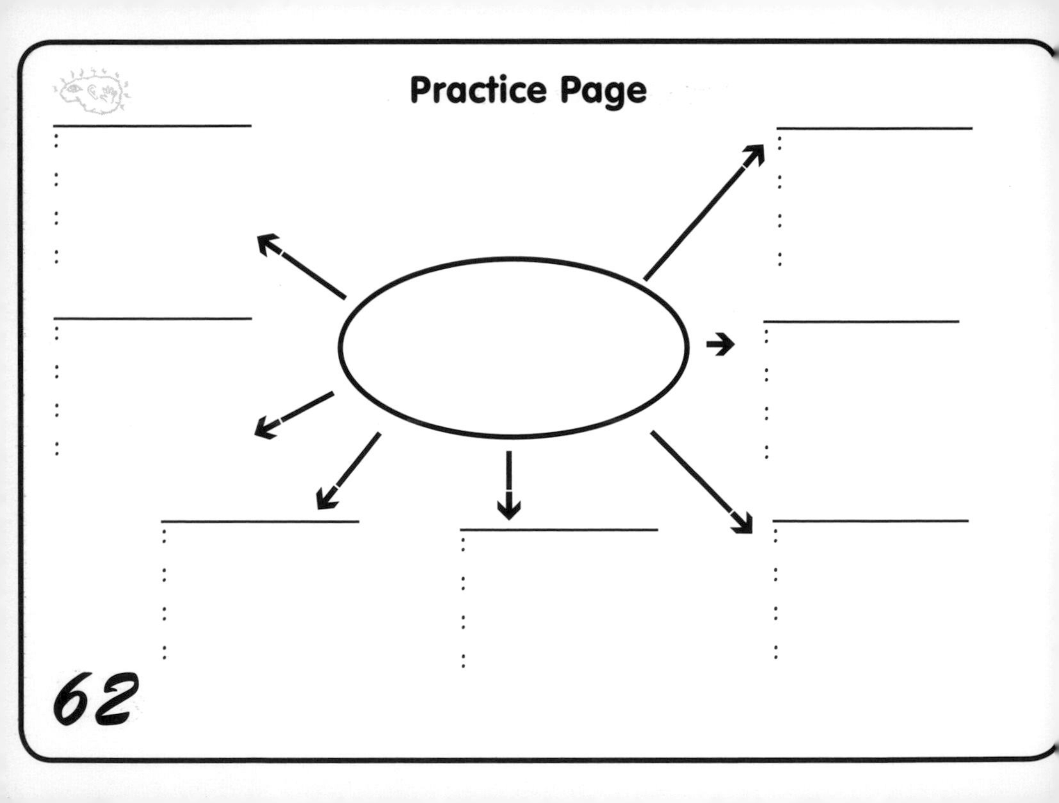

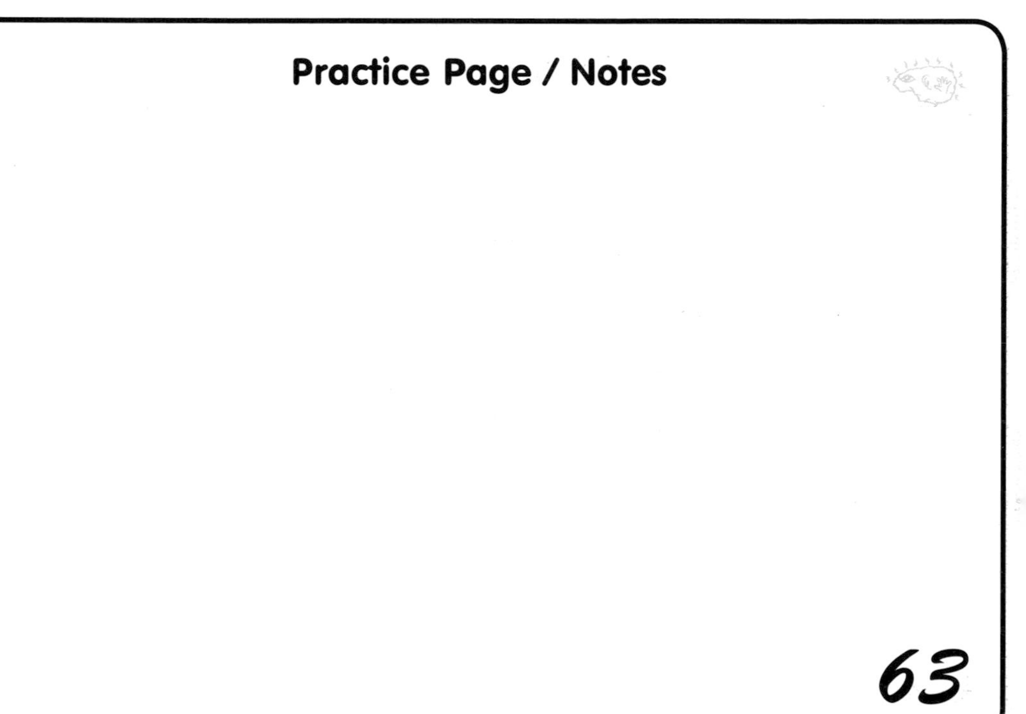

Practice Page / Notes

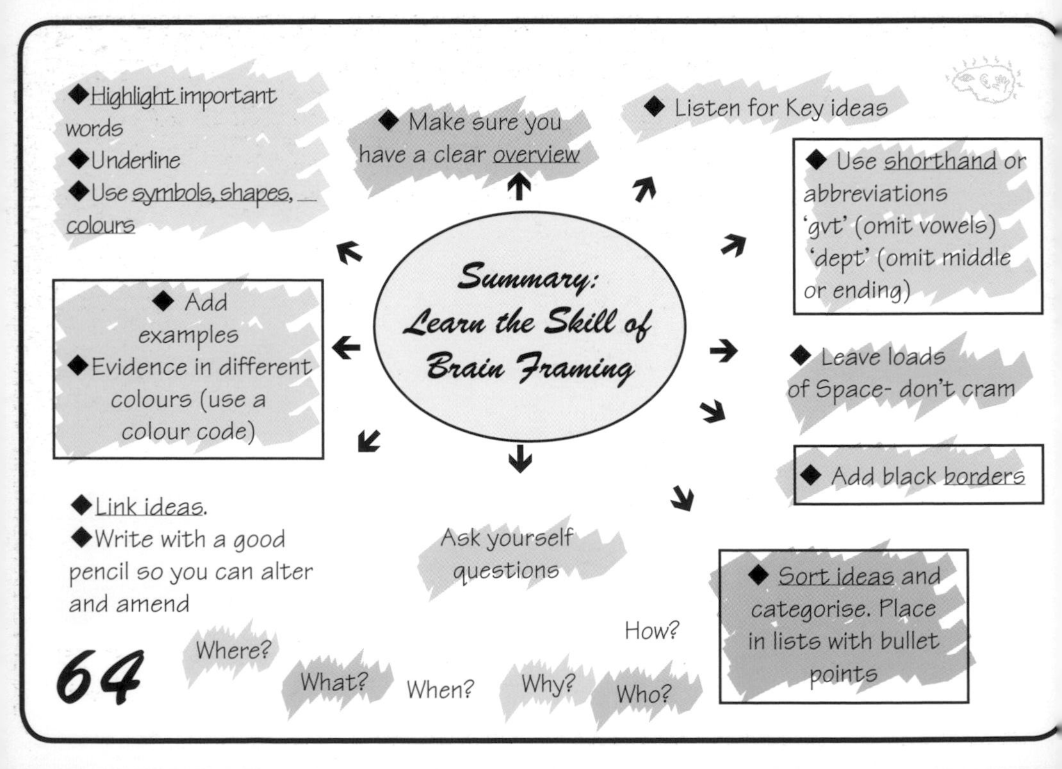
Summary: Learn the Skill of Brain Framing
◆ Highlight important words
◆ Underline
◆ Use symbols, shapes, colours
◆ Make sure you have a clear overview
◆ Listen for Key ideas
◆ Use shorthand or abbreviations 'gvt' (omit vowels) 'dept' (omit middle or ending)
◆ Add examples
◆ Evidence in different colours (use a colour code)
◆ Leave loads of Space- don't cram
◆ Add black borders
◆ Link ideas.
◆ Write with a good pencil so you can alter and amend
Ask yourself questions
◆ Sort ideas and categorise. Place in lists with bullet points
Where?
What?
When?
Why?
Who?
How?

Step 5 - Mind & Body Control

Each one of the following areas is as important to your success as Past Papers, Brainframes, clever memory tricks or perfect plans!

- Environment
- Diet / Vitamins
- Brain Exercise and Energy
- Fitness
- Building Concentration & Stamina

Take control of these and you will be relaxed yet focused. You will be stress-free and motivated!

Create a Successful Environment

Your work area is of considerable importance; it must be somewhere you feel at ease, motivated and positive.
Typical considerations are:

- Good lighting, balanced temperature (18°)
- A chair that matches your desk (discomfort will only cause interruptive anxiety and restricts blood supply to the brain)
- Shelving, power points, posters to back up your learning (we take in information subconciously and subliminally)
- Timetables and syllabus plans

Work in an area where you can leave your work undisturbed until you return

Diet and Vitamins

Diet in General - Too much sugar, starch, caffeine, alcohol and other uneccessary drugs leads to mental dullness. Keep a well balanced diet. Glucose generates 20/25 watts of electricity that enables the brain to function Do not skip meals, especially breakfast. Bananas and kiwi fruit increase potassium - good for thinking! Pasta, oats, muffins and so on. help release energy to your body more slowly, prolonging energy and stamina.

Vitamin A -	Aids Vision, found in fats and oils
B Vitamins -	Keep you mentally alert, found in wholegrains, seeds, lentils, yeast, nuts, eggs, and milk products
Vitamin B5 and B6	For memory, also found in fish and chicken - or fish oil tablets
Vitamin B3	Is essential for proper brain functioning
Vitamin B12	Is essential for the production of red blood cells, which carry oxygen (meat, milk and eggs).
Vitamin C -	Anti-Oxidant, protects other vitamins from destruction, found in fresh fruit and vegetables.
Vitamin E -	Increases cell oxygenation, found in wholegrains, wholewheat and sunflower seed oil

Be sure to consult your doctor before taking vitamins.
Avoid trendy “memory” or “concentration” pills - they don’t work!

"Brain Gym"

You will work faster and better if you:

Oxygenate the Brain & Adjust your Electrical Pathways

Put your thumb and index under your collar bone and massage the hollow.
It increases blood flow to the brain.

Open up your Brain Network

Put one ankle over the other knee, cross your hands the same way. Rest your tongue on the roof of your mouth and breath slowly. Think of a subject and let all you know about that subject flood back into your mind. This is an excellent exercise to do before a lesson or revision session. You remember what you already know in a relaxed way.

Release the Stress

You can switch off panic before every revision session and in exams. Above your eyebrows, on your forehead, are two neurovascular points. As you panic, blood rushes away from your thinking brain, causing mind blanks. By keeping your fingers pressed gently on these points, blood is encouraged to the front where your thinking takes place and you will be able to concentrate again. You can massage at the back of your head to help bring back visual images.

Fitness

General Exercise is Vital for Mind and Body

- Remember the brain uses 60% of body's oxygen and blood supply
- Controlled rhythmic breathing allows more oxygen to the brain.
- There is no best form of exercise - and it doesn't have to be painful
- Sleep and proper rest is essential for the brain to work at it's best
- Good cardiovascular function is vital for problem solving, concentration and stamina

Link Your Brains by Moving Your Body - Ambidextrous Activity

Your right hemisphere controls your left hand side of the body and left hemisphere controls the right side!

If you exercise by co-ordinating your right and left sides, you will be linking both brain hemispheres.

Try some co-ordinated movements before sitting down to study, because you'll concentrate faster and better.

Try juggling, aerobics, marching in time, doodling with both hands or bouncing a ball in both hands simultaneously!

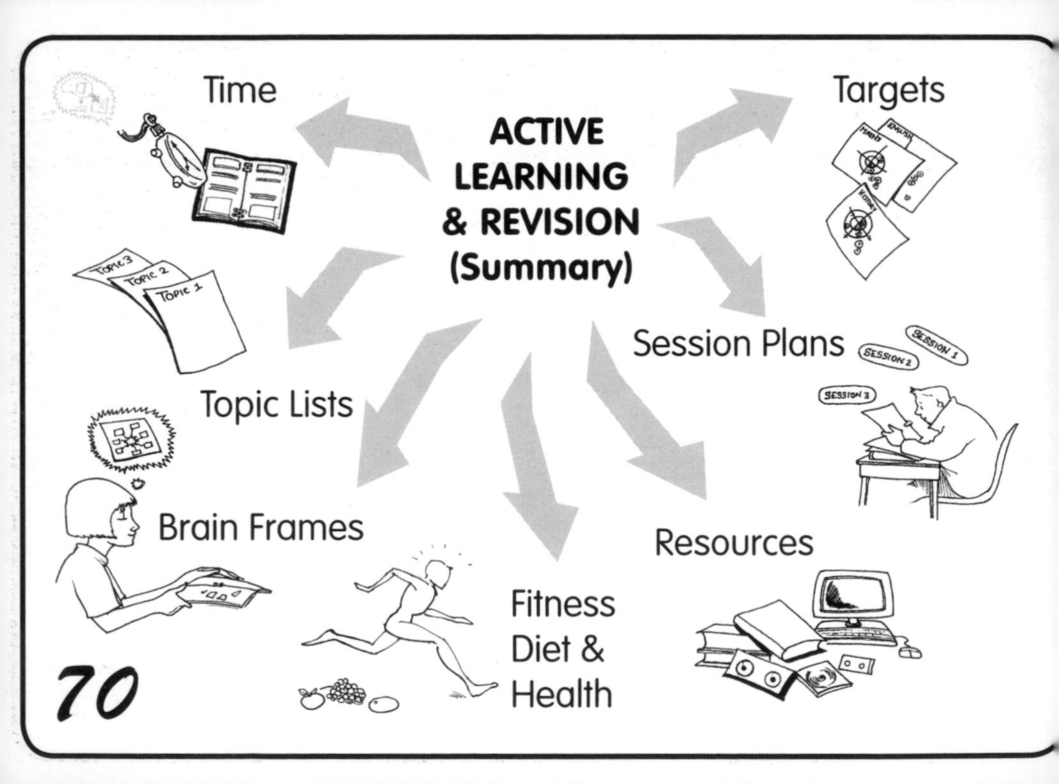
ACTIVE LEARNING & REVISION (Summary)
Time
Targets
MATHS
ENGLISH
HISTORY
TOPIC 3
TOPIC 2
TOPIC 1
Topic Lists
Session Plans
SESSION 1
SESSION 2
SESSION 3
Brain Frames
Resources
Fitness Diet & Health

Step 6 - Memorising & Making Sure

Everything we've covered so far relates to 'revision'. This particular section specifically relates to the actual subject skills and exam answers, both in planning format and in style. This is:
Exam Preparation - Showing You Know Part I

Multi Sensory Subject Skills

↓

Defining Answers

↓

SKANSAS ← Planning, Writing & Checkin

↓

Exam Answers

Multi-Sensory Intelligences & Subject Revision Skills

General Skills. Remember - it's the use of all senses frequently that builds memory.

- Overviews
- Brain frames
- Tapes / Audio
- Topic lists
- Lists of Questions
- Types and styles
- Example answers
- Sketch answers
- Posters
- Filing notes
- 'Chunking' of pics into manageable sizes
- Answer Multi Questions - who, what, why, when, what, how
- Flash cards

Business Studies

- Brainframing
- Overviews
- Visualise
- Role Play
- Case studies
- 'Models' - diagrams
- Create comparisons

Design Technology

- Dictionary / glossary of terms and definitions
- Annotate Brain frames of syllabus
- Collect information - cuttings, diagrams etc.
- Scrap book / Folder. Very visual notes
- Practice the activity.
- Visualise practicals, experiments, fixings, fittings, etc.

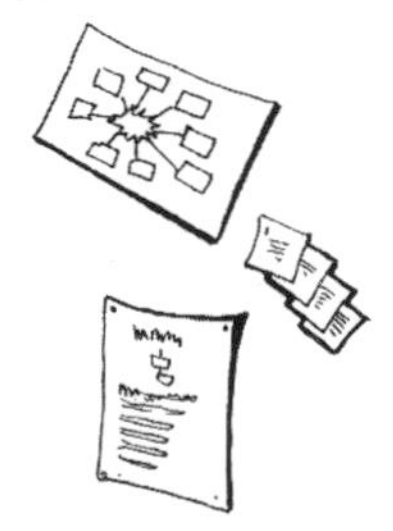

Drama or English:

- Brain frames
- Selection of Key Ideas
- Sumarising
- Flow chart of events
- Visual depictions
- List Key Spellings
- Lists of Quotations
- Question planning
- Discussions
- Reading aloud
- Examples of Style/Genre
- Lists of link words
- Audio tapes
- Role play
- Proof Reading
- Text / colour codes annotation
- Theatre trips

Geography

- Glossary of terms
- Brainframes
- Overviews including case studies / models
- Practice papers
- Simple models / make posters

Languages:

◆Vocabulary lists ◆Visual learners need to visualise word or scene
◆Look, cover, write, check.
◆Listen to the spoken word (Revision - Audio tapes)
◆Reading comprehensions - participate (Revision Audio - tapes)
◆Make your own audio tapes
◆Words within wods "mal-heureux" or similar English words "equipe - equipment
◆Speak aloud a lot! Imitate others
◆Write out a lot - sentences - syntax / grammar (verbs / nouns etc.)
◆Constant reviews ◆Practical learners will need role play

History / R.E

◆Overviews of events / timecharts - 'whole picture' is vital - creates "event, issues & evidence" chart
◆Lists of selected facts - in chunks
◆Simple posters - maps - flow chart for progression and obvious links
◆Visual images ◆Comparisons, similarities, differences
◆Advantages & disadvantages
◆Case studies / Examples
◆Discuss, teach & test
◆Multi-Question -why, who, what, when, where, how?

Maths:

- ◆Basic examples of topics - simple 1st
- ◆Define terms - prime no, squareno, formulas
- ◆Practice answers, build up to complicated.
- ◆Create a game
- ◆Accumulate Knowledge from basics
- ◆Visual examples / models / charts
- ◆Physical Models
- ◆Flash cards / posters of formulae
- ◆Work up to topics that mix skills & other topics

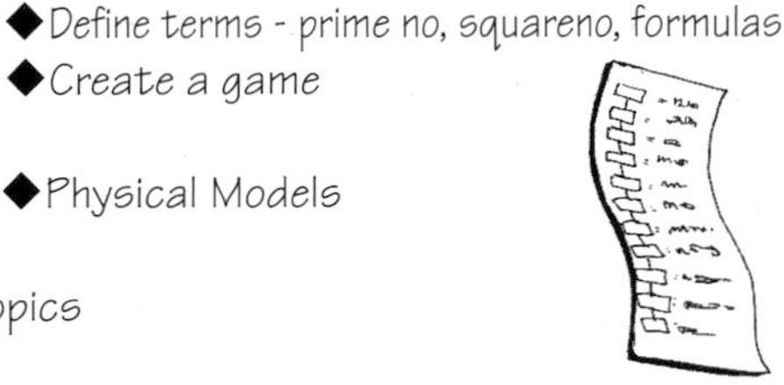

Sciences

- ◆Separate into Biology, Chemistry & Physics
- ◆List topics: overview Brain Frames
- ◆Practice drawing & labelling diagrams
- ◆Define rules :acid + alkali gives salt + water
- ◆Charts / posters / flash cards; formulae and models
- ◆Work around visual images
- ◆Lists and flow charts to show progression
- ◆Work around visual images
- ◆Try to see where topics overlap / imitate with each other
- ◆Look for associations "photosynthesis=photo=light"

START SIMPLY! Use brainframes and add information from time to time. Do not rely on 'Revision' books alone, but knowledge from a variety of sources. Go through 'Brain Framer' steps to encourage whole brain repetition and to activate working brain cell connections.

The Answer

All your work will require you to SOLVE PROBLEMS or find answers to solutions. These require critical Thinking Skills - the ability to 'process' or work out an answer. We always recommend this mnemonic:

A **A**sk whats wanted - Define the Question

N **N**otes - create Brainframes - 'Skydiver' & 'Explorer' details

S **S**keleton Answer - Sketch out the 'route' you need to take

W **W**rite it

E **E**valuate and Edit as you go

R **R**eview it

See 'The Great Little Book of Brainpower' for more details; pp 110 - 114

Definition and Interpretation

All Questions have COMMAND words (see the next two pages). You must know what they mean and be used to defining them well before the exams.
They may vary a bit from subject to subject so ask for advice on this:

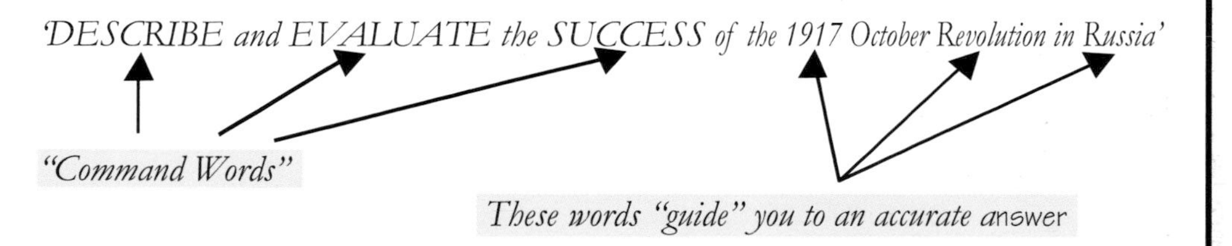

It is commonly the case that as much as 30% of students who underachieve in some exams do so because they fail to interpret the Question correctly.

Typical 'Command' Words in questions

You must know these to be able to understand what's really wanted

ANALYSE	Give main ideas, connections and importance
ASSESS	Give weak or strong points
AVERAGE	The middle
CALCULATE	Find the answer (Maths)
COMMENT ON	Say what you think
COMPARE	Point out similarities
CONTRAST	Show difference between two things
CRITICIZE	Say what you think for and against
DEFINE	Give the meaning
DESCRIBE	Write a picture in words
DIAGRAM	Make a drawing, graph or chart
DIFFERENTIATE	Say precise differences
DISCUSS	Write in detail
DISTINGUISH	Differences between
ENUMERATE	List
ESSENTIAL	Most important
EVALUATE	Give good and bad points about a subject
EVIDENCE	Proof: facts

EXAMINE	Investigate pros and cons and explain
EXPLAIN	Give clear answers
XPRESS	Say a different way (maths)
ILLUSTRATE	Use examples to make a point
INTERPRET	Show what it means
JUSTIFY	Explain your answer
OPTION	A choice
OUTLINE	A sketch in words of the main idea
PATH	Explain answer step by step
PICTORIAL	In a picture
PURPOSE	The reason why
RELATE	Show connections
REQUIREMENT	Thing to be done
REVIEW	Overall view
STATE	Write in brief
STRUGGLE	Work out answer based on Knowledge
SUMMARIZE	Pull together main points
TRACE	Tell the history

Check these definitions with those that teach you for they may differ slightly from subject to subject.

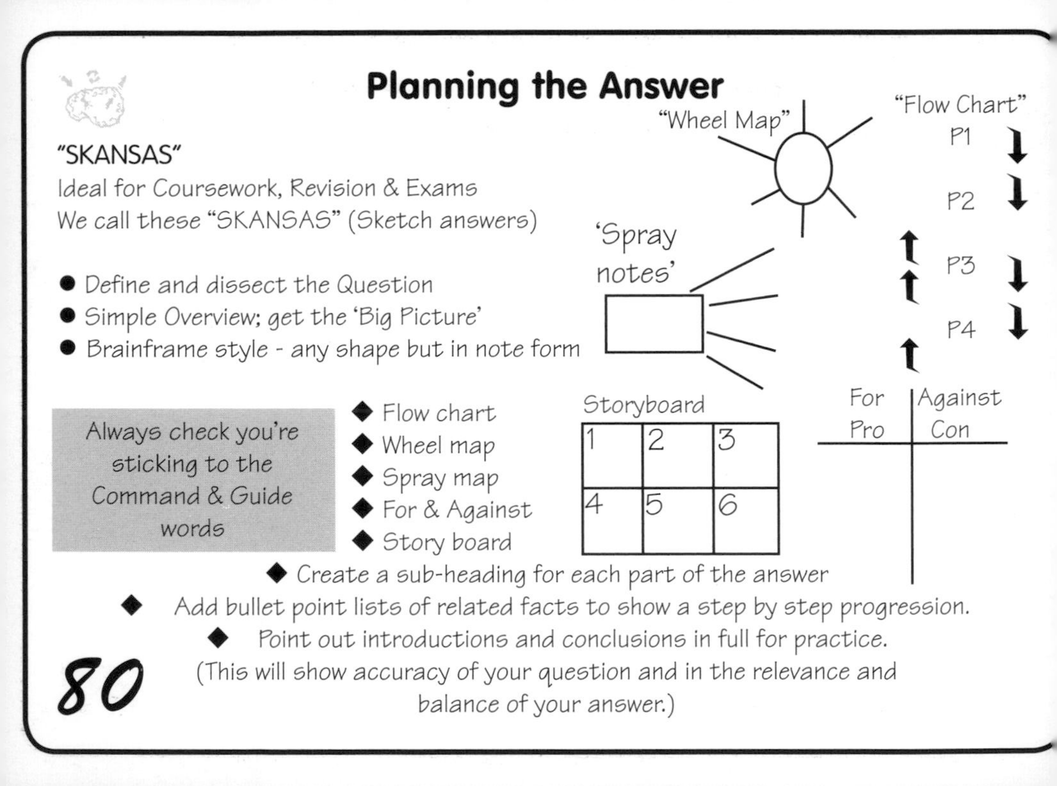
Planning the Answer
"SKANSAS"
Ideal for Coursework, Revision & Exams
We call these "SKANSAS" (Sketch answers)
● Define and dissect the Question
● Simple Overview; get the 'Big Picture'
● Brainframe style - any shape but in note form
"Wheel Map"
"Flow Chart"
P1
P2
P3
P4
'Spray notes'
Always check you're sticking to the Command & Guide words
◆ Flow chart
◆ Wheel map
◆ Spray map
◆ For & Against
◆ Story board
Storyboard
1
2
3
4
5
6
For
Pro
Against
Con
◆ Create a sub-heading for each part of the answer
◆ Add bullet point lists of related facts to show a step by step progression.
◆ Point out introductions and conclusions in full for practice.
(This will show accuracy of your question and in the relevance and balance of your answer.)
80

Planning - Including Timing

Visual plans allow for the whole brain to become involved.

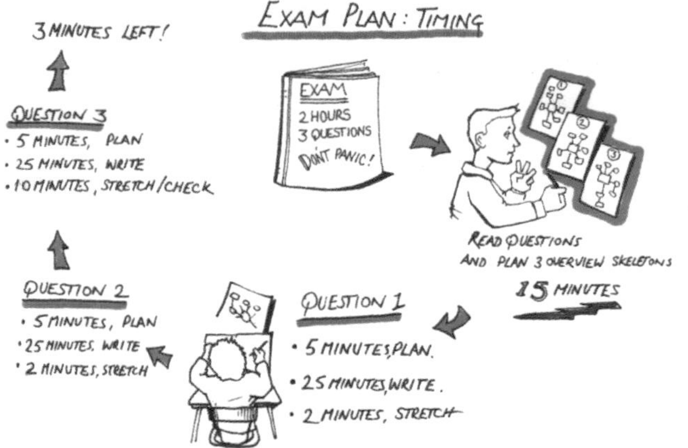

You will visual plans easier to:

- See the procession from the problem posed to the solution (answer)
- Stick to the question - (remain relevant)
- Stick to timings
- See comparisons / create links

Example SKANSA

INTRO

'It could be argued that the Russian revolution of October 1917 was merely caused by economic hardships forced upon the Russian people by the war with Germany, but it is possible to discover disturbing trends towards revolution from as early as the end of the C19th...'

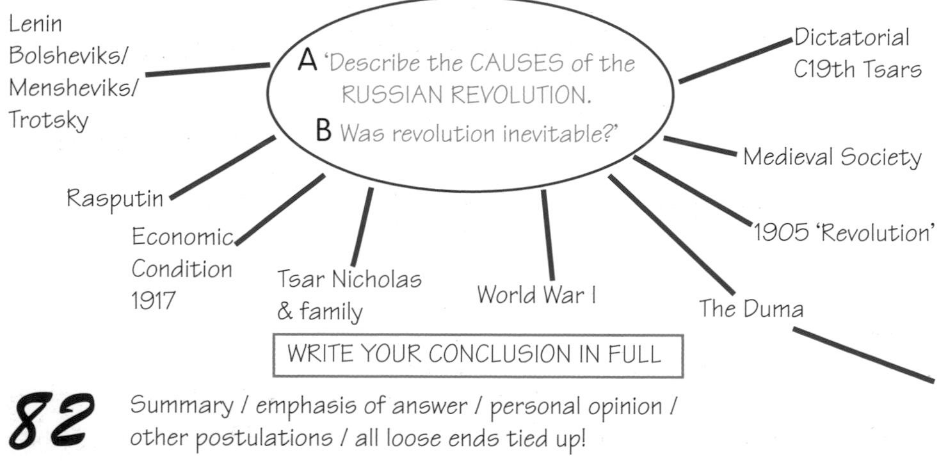

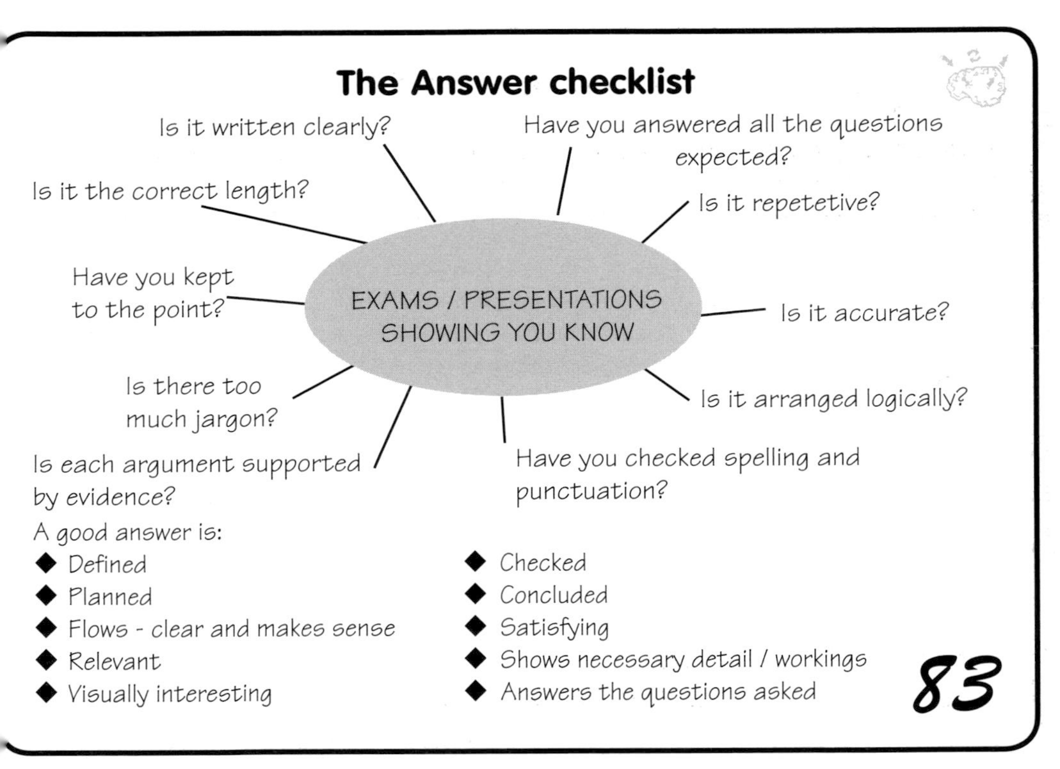
The Answer checklist
Is it written clearly?
Have you answered all the questions expected?
Is it the correct length?
Is it repetetive?
Have you kept to the point?
EXAMS / PRESENTATIONS SHOWING YOU KNOW
Is it accurate?
Is there too much jargon?
Is it arranged logically?
Is each argument supported by evidence?
Have you checked spelling and punctuation?
A good answer is:
◆ Defined
◆ Planned
◆ Flows - clear and makes sense
◆ Relevant
◆ Visually interesting
◆ Checked
◆ Concluded
◆ Satisfying
◆ Shows necessary detail / workings
◆ Answers the questions asked
83

Multi Sensory Memory and Intelligences

On page 11 you can see the "model" of how Multi Sensory Learning can place information and experience in your Long Term Memory. Here are the steps required:

Use all your senses and intelligences (p9-13)
Plan a logical strategy - chunk, lists, spot connections (Maths/logical intelligence)
Mnemonics, chanting, rhyme, tapes (Musical intelligence)
Games, cartoons & "trigger" sentences (Creative intelligence)
Posters, Brainframes, flashcards, visualisation (Visual / spatial intelligence)
Teach someone else (Interpersonal intelligence)
Create relaxed, positive mindstate
Reflect & plan improvement
Intend to remember (Intrapersonal intelligence)
Linguistic skills - write it, stories
analogies (Language intelligence)
Role play, draw, mime
Make games (Practical intelligence)

What Your Memory Really, Really wants ...

Good Memory and remembering MUST have the following:

- TRIGGERS...Why do you think advertising is so successful?
  They trigger thoughts, memories, 'feel good' and associated facts.

- NO MORE THAN 7 AREAS/FACTS/ITEMS...learnt in one session.
  (Plus or minus one depending on your preference).

- EMOTIONAL LINKS...Funny, unusual, silly, weird - even crude!
  Your middle LTM brain likes this!.

- VISUAL IMAGES CREATED BY YOU...
  Drawings, imagined mental movies.

- ASSOCIATIONS...Connections, similarities.

What Your Memory Really, Really wants ...

(Continued)

- RETAIN...Organised items. Multi - sensory input.
- REVIEW...Check understanding and clear RECEPTION.
- REINFORCE...repetitive, short, little and often...REMINDERS.
- RECALL...Test yourself. Teach someone else.
- RETRIEVE...Under pressure (Triggers and visual images).
- REHEARSE...Regularly overview every few weeks- a few minutes at a time. Use it or lose it!

Memory Techniques II

Alphabet System (Max 7 items at a time)

the peg word must start with the sound of the letter, e.g

A = Ace not Apple, C = Sea not Cat:

A = Ale
B = Bee
C = Sea
D = Dead
E = Easel
F = Effluent
G =Gee Gee
H = H-Bomb
I = Eye

If you want to remember the word "bag" you would visualise a bee drinking ale on a horse!

PEG SYSTEMS (Number Shapes)

1 = Sword
2 = Snake
3 = Hills
4 = Boat
5 = Hook

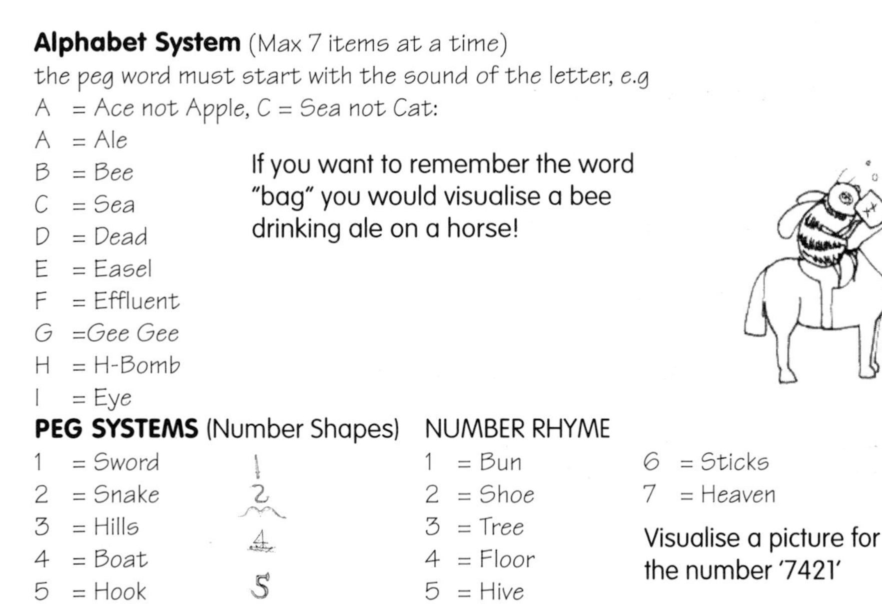

NUMBER RHYME

1 = Bun
2 = Shoe
3 = Tree
4 = Floor
5 = Hive
6 = Sticks
7 = Heaven

Visualise a picture for the number '7421'

Number Rhymes - Memory Techniques III

Location / Room Systems: assign places / objects around your room to a list of facts (preferably in sequence) that you have to learn.
i.e "WW1 Trenches"

Mud	Gas	Raids
Duck boards	Wire	Shells
Trench foot	Snipers	Machine Guns

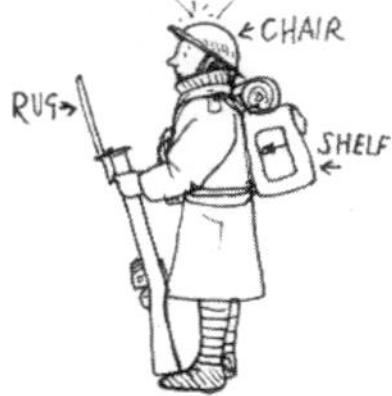

Link System: Visualisation.
Form a vivid picture of each item you read to learn... then link them together into a sequence or a story.

Try this:

Elephant	Jelly	Umbrella
Bus Stop	Frog	Bicycle

Step 7 - Showing You Know 2

This section deals with the actual exam period up to 4-6 weeks. Remember, if you have followed the rest of the advice in this little book, you will be familiar with a lot of these practices already.

- Days running up to exam period
- The day
- In the exam - Instructions
- The unexpected. Dealing with anxiety
- Looking after yourself
- After the exam
- Learning Advisors

Exam Period

The days leading up to the exam period (14-21 days)

- Plan your sessions carefully - always ask yourself 'What do I still need to do? How can I improve? ; 'How would I answer questions on....'
- Check all equipment - plan your supplies. (watch, energy booster, water, calculator, etc.) especially the night before an exam.
- Allow yourself plenty of relaxation time - practise controlling stress. Plan some 'review' sessions to reassure yourself that you're in control.
- Don't revise late in the evening - your final 'intense' session should not be after 8.00 p.m
- Find somewhere to exercise, you will need to unwind and work off stress.
- Talk to others and ask for help if you're anxious.
- Find a way to laugh - laughter releases tension.

In the evening

- Overview your topic (2-5 mins each).
- Have plenty of relaxation. Try to clear your mind.

Then:
- Sleep (you need 8 hours).

Night before:

- Overview your topic.
- Relax, don't work late.
- Don't try to learn new stuff!
- Go over typical SKANAS
- Check:

  Timings

  Venue / travel arrangements

On the Day

- Get up slightly earlier than usual to allow your brain to fully wake up.
- Set off slightly earlier - arrive at the exam room about 10 minutes before (not too early - avoid the panic people.)
- Check desk, chair, equipment.
- Relax. Focus on your topic. Try some Brain excercises. Drink water and have the essential 'brain booster' (if permitted)

Following Instructions:

- Listen to the Invigilator. (There can be changes to instructions.)
- Fill in Examination Centre details and your name.
- Read written instructions carefully, they will tell you: time; choice of questions; type of answer; number of marks.
- Read all the questions. Eliminate those you don't want to do.
- Choose very carefully because each question deserves time - you may suddenly realise you **can** do it after all.
- Plan as you've been practising all along.

Plans and Time

WHAT HAPPENS IF YOU DON'T PLAN YOUR TIME?

- You rush answers and panic.
- You leave out answers or miss obvious questions.
- Your memory doesn't react - so you begin to feel worried.

WHAT HAPPENS IF YOU FALL BEHIND IN YOUR PLAN?

- Don't panic: reduce each answer time - you CAN do it!
- Go into note form if absolutely necessary.
- **Finish** EACH question - show your working out if you have to.

Dealing with the Unexpected

What happens if you're mind goes blank and you begin to panic?

Remember how your brain works. If you allow yourself to panic you will 'squeeze' out access to your memory.

What to do if you feel panic:

- relaxation techniques do help - stretch; take deep breaths; rub the neurovascular points on your forehead
- don't spend too long trying to remember a point - leave a space or line. Come back to it later.
- keep writing any thoughts on rough paper ask yourself questions - who, why, where, when, how, what happened, what resulted? Then try again. You often know more than you think you do!

Remember you do know it. If it is a very difficult question relax and resolve to give your best. Once you are calmer it is amazing how you will suddenly remember the information you need

Looking After Yourself in the Exam

- Make sure the chair is comfortable. Stretch arms, fingers and legs to encourage blood flow.
- Drink water - take some supplies (small amount of chocolate or peppermints activate the synapses?)
- Do something ambidextrous (double doodles)
- Activate neurovascular points.
- Give yourself 1-2 minute breaks
- Smile - even if it's tough!

Post mortems

Should you go through an exam immediately afterwards to assess your success rate? On balance, no. You do gain plenty of reassurance if you've done well. But if you discover you've done badly (And you may be wrong!) you will be demotivated and it will possibly affect how you do in other exams.

Look to the future and don't spend time getting worked up about the past. What's done is done!

The Benefits of Having a Learning Advisor

All of our research has shown that Learners achieve more if they have a non-judgemental advisor. (coach, mentor, consultant)

- You can show concern / worries and receive understanding
- You can seek help / ideas
- You can gain structure / organisation
- They can help you have an objective view and balance your work and play
- They can help motivate, plan and support you without needing to judge you.
- They can liaise with teachers and your family

They are always available to you.

Try this sort of Supporter

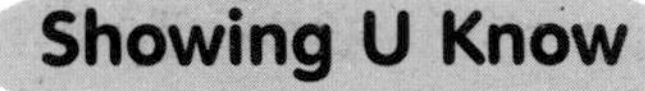

MEMORY SKILLS

POSITIVE ANSWERS

STAYING CALM & IN CONTROL

PLANNING

CAREFUL PREPARATION DAYS BEFORE